A Glut of Courgettes & Marrows

Ann Carr

*Illustrated by
Martin MacKeown*

MEREHURST PRESS
LONDON

*The Publishers wish to thank
Rosemary Wilkinson and Malcolm Saunders
for their help with this book.*

First published 1988 by Merehurst Press
5 Great James Street
London WC1N 3DA

Produced by
Malcolm Saunders Publishing Ltd
26 Ornan Road, London NW3 4QB

Copyright © 1988 this edition
Malcolm Saunders Publishing Ltd
Copyright © 1988 text Ann Carr
Copyright © 1988 design
and illustrations Martin MacKeown

ISBN 0 948075 86 4

Photoset in Linotype Ehrhardt
by Fakenham Photosetting Limited
Printed in Spain

CONTENTS

FOREWORD

If ever fruits and vegetables have been ruined by their reputation for sheer size, they are the unfortunate marrow and pumpkin: the bigger they grew the better they were thought to be. When they had become truly vast, tough-skinned and tasteless, they were carted off to the village fête or local gardening competition where bets were placed on their weight and prizes given for their huge growth. It is hardly surprising that they were little used in the kitchen for, by that time and at such a size, they were only fit for magic lanterns or for turning into a coach for a Cinderella.

But, thank goodness, times and tastes have changed and gardening catalogues are now full of exciting new varieties of squash,

9

pumpkin and gourd. Supermarkets, greengrocers and local markets have summer and autumn displays of green, orange and tawny-yellow squashes and pumpkins. The large varieties are often cut up for sale and wrapped in clear cellophane, so that the cook can buy small portions to experiment with. Courgettes/zucchini, once rare, are now the most common variety of squash. These vegetables are fast gaining in popularity and, consistent with our changing eating pattern involving a reduced consumption of meat and fats, are a welcome addition to the table.

Once the glut season is over, it is still possible to find squashes, pumpkins and edible gourds in specialist greengrocers and, although these are not quite the same varieties as those covered here, they can be used in your favourite squash recipes.

Crookneck

INTRODUCTION

Cucurbitaceae is the botanical name for marrows, squashes, pumpkins and gourds – a large family of fruits and vegetables that also includes cucumbers, gherkins, melons and chayotes/chokos. This book deals with one section of the family members, namely those we call squashes and pumpkins, embracing marrows, courgettes/zucchini, butternuts and edible gourds.

The naming of these fruits or vegetables is not easy; for what or which is a pumpkin or squash? These names do not refer to a specific plant type and are merely names of convenience rather than of botanical accuracy. To complicate things further, that which is called a pumpkin in Australia is known as a squash in the USA. Shape and colour don't help much either: there are pumpkins which look like squashes and vice-versa. The English vegetable marrow is just one of the many varieties of summer squash.

It is important to note that winter squashes are not a winter cropping variety but squashes

Vegetable Marrow

that will store for use during the winter
months.

This table should help:

Summer Squashes

England	Australia	USA
vegetable marrow	*vegetable marrow*	*squash or marrow squash*
courgette	*zucchini*	*zucchini*

Winter Squashes

England	Australia	USA
pumpkin	*pumpkin*	*squash*

Perhaps the easiest way, though it is very
general, is to group them by their culinary
use. Pumpkins generally have coarser-
textured, stronger-flavoured flesh than

squashes and therefore are rarely used as vegetables but are turned into the famous pie or into pumpkin soups. Squashes, on the other hand, have a finer-grained, more subtly-flavoured flesh and are commonly used as table vegetables; the modern squash being a far cry from the old, overgrown vegetable that appeared, soggy, tepid and smothered under a grim and stiff white sauce, on our winter table.

These members of the cucurbitaceae family are thought to have originated in South America and didn't appear in Europe until the sixteenth century, when Tusser mentioned them in his writings.

The most common varieties in use today belong to one of three species of cucurbitaceae. They are *cucurbita maxima*, *cucurbita pepo* and *cucurbita moschata*. This is not as simple as it seems for there are both squash and pumpkin cultivars belonging to each of

Pumpkin

these species. For our purposes it is not necessary to go further into the botanical divisions and sub-divisions: it is easier to divide them into understandable culinary and garden terms.

Squashes

These members of the cucurbita family are divided into two distinct groups: Summer and Winter Squashes.

Summer squashes (generally bush culti-vars) include those cultivars that not only are best eaten young but do not grow tough enough skins for long-term storage. The fruits should be picked very young, two to three days after the flower blooms. This not only gives wonderful, tender fruits but also allows more fruit to develop and so produces an overall higher yield. Some well-known favourites are courgette/zucchini, dawn, scallop or patty-pan squashes (which come in greeny white turning to chalk white at 6 in (15 cm) or yellow varieties) and Little Gem – this last will store for a short time. The scallop squashes are best when no big-ger than shallow teacup size and courgettes/zucchini ideal at 4 to 5 in (10 to 12 cm). It is interesting to note that most of the summer squashes come under the *cucurbita pepo* classification.

Winter squashes in general seem to fall into the *cucurbita maxima* grouping. These squashes have a longer growing season than the summer cultivars and are harvested when mature. They are largely of trailing habit and need more growing space than bush cultivars. Whenever possible, let the fruit ripen fully before harvesting. In a warm, dry climate, an outdoor 'curing' period is necessary before long-term storage. This is usually done by leaving them out in the field for eight to ten days after cutting but do cover at night if in a frosty area. The familiar cultivars are Argentina marrow, Butterkist and Butternut, Baby Blue, Golden Delicious, Hubbard, Turk's Turban, Queensland Blue, onion

Turk's Turban

squash, acorn squash and also Little Gem which falls into both winter and summer categories.

Pumpkins

Until recently the pumpkin was out of fashion in our gardens and kitchens. It is in the same category as the summer squash, *cucurbita pepo*, and is eaten when large and mature. However, unlike winter squash, it has a relatively smooth skin. Usually the plant is of a trailing variety but some bush and 'compact vine' cultivars are available.

Most pumpkins mature in the autumn and if grown in a frost area should be protected and, if necessary, picked and stored away from frost, where they will ripen and, if in good condition, will keep well.

Pumpkins can be grouped by size. Between 5 and 8 lb (2 to 4 kg) they are commonly called pie pumpkins. The 9 to 15 pounders (5 to 8 kg) are particularly suited to English growing conditions. The 'big boys', which range from 15 to 25 lb (8 to 12 kg), are

17

mainly used for decoration. Some of the pumpkin names express well their association with Hallowe'en, fairy tales, or just their size. In the 5 to 8 lb (2 to 4 kg) range, there is a variety called Spookie, in the 9 to 15 pounders (5 to 8 kg) range come Cinderella and Jack O'Lantern, and the huge pumpkins have such names as Big Max, Mammoth Gourd, Atlantic Giant and Hungarian Mammoth. All but the very large ones are worth experimenting with in the kitchen.

Chayote/Choko

No recipes are given for this tropical squash but it is available in some greengrocers and you might like to try experimenting. It has a slightly prickly skin and contains one large edible seed. It is best boiled whole for 50 minutes to one hour, sliced in half, then stuffed with a favourite savoury stuffing. Next, dot with butter or drizzle with oil and cook at 190 °C (375 °F/Gas 5) for 15 to 20 minutes. Serve with plain boiled rice.

Telling tales of the fairy who travelled like
   steam,
In a pumpkin-shell coach, with two rats for her
   team!
   (1844, John Greenleaf Whittier 'Pumpkin')

Olive oil

Where olive oil is listed in the ingredients, try to use the best available and avoid using alternative cooking oils, as these will not enhance the flavour of the dish in the same, subtle way.

Garlic

Garlic that is to be cooked quickly is much better chopped finely than crushed or minced which is more appropriate for salads and dressings.

COOKS' NOTES

1. Unless specific details are given in the individual recipes, the following apply:

– spoon measurements are level

– sugar is granulated

– eggs are standard size

2. Follow either the imperial measurements or the metric but do not mix them, as they have been calculated separately.

3. As individual oven temperatures vary, use the timings in the recipes as a guide. Always preheat your oven or grill.

The Recipes

COURGETTES/ZUCCHINI

If you are using your own home-grown courgettes/zucchini, pick them as young as possible. When buying, choose courgettes/zucchini that are firm with tight glossy skins, the smaller the better. It is not usually necessary to peel courgettes/zucchini. Occasionally, when older or grown in too cold a climate, the skins can be bitter; in which case scrape lightly with a sharp knife, rinse and dry. Unskinned courgettes/zucchini need only a wipe with a clean, damp cloth to remove soil or the slight fuzz that some varieties have.

Marinated Courgettes/ Zucchini

This is a refreshing summer starter. Young courgettes/zucchini are best.

Serves 4
4 fl oz (125 ml) olive oil
1 fl oz (30 ml) fresh lemon juice
1 clove garlic, crushed
1 tablespoon fresh parsley, chopped
1 tablespoon fresh basil, roughly chopped
salt and pepper, to taste
1½ lb (750 g) young courgettes/zucchini, wiped clean
2 firm tomatoes, peeled, seeded and chopped

Place oil, lemon juice, garlic, herbs, salt and pepper in a screw-topped jar and shake well to combine. Slice courgettes/zucchini diagonally into 1½–2 in (4–5 cm) lengths, place in a steamer and steam for 3 to 4 minutes, they must be very firm. If you do not have a steamer, sweat with 2 to 3 tablespoons of water in a heavy pan covered with a tight-fitting lid, shaking frequently to prevent burning. Drain quickly and at once, then, while courgettes/zucchini are still hot, pour over vinaigrette. Leave to cool, then add tomatoes.

Courgettes/Zucchini

Courgettes/Zucchini with Tomato & Garlic

The quantities used in this recipe are flexible, depending on what you have available but it is best made with very fresh courgettes/zucchini. Though quick and simple to make, it does require last-minute cooking and cannot be kept waiting, making it particularly suited to family suppers.

Serves 4–6
1–1½ lb (500–750 g) courgettes/
zucchini
2–3 fl oz (60–90 ml) olive oil
3–4 cloves garlic, finely chopped
2–3 large tomatoes, peeled and chopped
salt and freshly ground black pepper, to
taste

Wipe courgettes/zucchini clean and slice into ¼ in (0.5 cm) rounds. Heat olive oil in a large frying pan, add garlic and courgettes/zucchini and stir-fry over a medium heat for 4 to 5 minutes. The courgettes/zucchini should colour quite a bit. Add tomatoes, salt and pepper, increase heat if necessary and stir-fry for a further 3 to 4 minutes until tomatoes are thoroughly heated. Do not overcook, the courgettes/zucchini should be crisp and the tomatoes very fresh tasting. Serve at once.

Courgettes/Zucchini in Tomato Sauce

This is good with a pasta dish.

Serves 4–5

1½ lb (750 g) courgettes/zucchini

2 fl oz (60 ml) olive oil

1 clove garlic, chopped

10 fl oz (315 ml) Fresh Tomato Sauce, see page 84

salt and pepper, to taste

1 tablespoon chopped fresh parsley, to finish or 2 tablespoons fried breadcrumbs

Wipe courgettes/zucchini clean and cut in half lengthwise. Heat olive oil in a large frying pan, add garlic and courgettes/zucchini and gently stir-fry for 3 to 4 minutes. Remove and arrange in an ovenproof dish. Pour over the tomato sauce to which you have added salt and pepper. Place in the oven at 180–190 °C (350–375 °F/Gas 4–5) for 15 to 20 minutes, until the sauce bubbles and the courgettes/zucchini are cooked but still firm. Sprinkle with parsley or breadcrumbs and serve.

He behelde a fruyt rycht feire and swete 'Gourdys' thus men clepe ye name.

> *(1303, Robert Manning Brunne 'Handling Synne')*

Deep-Fried Courgettes/ Zucchini

This is a recipe for older courgettes/ zucchini. You will need 1 to 2 courgettes/ zucchini per person, depending on their size.

Wipe the courgettes/zucchini clean and slice into ¼ in (0.5 cm) slices. Place in a colander, sprinkle lightly with salt, then toss gently and leave for an hour to exude any bitter juices. Rinse well and pat dry with a clean tea towel. Place 2 to 3 tablespoons plain flour in a plastic bag, add a few of the courgettes/zucchini pieces, shake well, remove and place quickly into a deep frying pan which contains 1 to 2 in (3 to 5 cm) of very hot oil, or deep fry in a deep fat fryer. Fry for 3 to 4 minutes, turning frequently, drain and serve at once. These are especially good served with a tomato sauce, or try a sauce rémoulade.

Courgettes/Zucchini Plain Boiled & Divine

This recipe really applies only to the tiniest courgettes/zucchini you can buy or have the courage to pick; they should be no bigger than a pea-pod. You will need:

3–4 courgettes/zucchini per person, more for the greedy

3–4 fl oz (90–125 ml) vinaigrette (3 parts best olive oil to 1 part wine vinegar) or 3–4 oz (90–125 g) butter (for 4 people)

freshly ground black pepper, to taste

Wipe courgettes/zucchini clean and, if you like, trim off the orange tips left by the flowers, though leaving these on shows how very young and tender the courgettes/zucchini are. Bring a pan of water to the boil, add salt and the courgettes/zucchini and hard boil for 2 to 3 minutes. Drain, quickly slice lengthwise, then place in a warm dish and pour over vinaigrette or butter. Add freshly ground black pepper and serve at once. Do not be tempted to add any herbs or garlic to this dish.

We dined on Indian corn and squash soop, and boiled bread.

(1751, John Bartram 'Observations in his Travels from Pennsylvania')

Courgettes/Zucchini with Currants & Pine Nuts

A quick stir-fry dish with a Middle-Eastern flavour.

1 lb (500 g) firm courgettes/zucchini
1 fl oz (30 ml) olive oil
2 spring onions, chopped
1 tablespoon pine nuts
2 tablespoons currants
1 tablespoon chopped fresh mint
salt and pepper, to taste

Wipe courgettes/zucchini and grate on the largest holes of a grater, or slice wafer thin on a mandoline or in a food processor. Heat oil in a frying pan, add courgettes/zucchini together with all the other ingredients and stir-fry for 3 to 4 minutes, until thoroughly heated through and just cooked. Serve at once.

Courgettes/Zucchini in a Soufflé

This is hardly likely to use up masses of courgettes/zucchini but made as a main course it is delicious and sustaining: all you need to accompany it is a good tomato salad.

Serves 3

4–6 courgettes/zucchini, depending on size
1 oz (30 g) butter
1 oz (30 g) flour
8 fl oz (250 ml) milk
3 eggs, separated
1 tablespoon chopped fresh parsley
salt and freshly ground black pepper, to taste

Wipe and slice courgettes/zucchini finely, using a mandoline or food processor. Melt butter in a saucepan over a gentle heat, add flour and stir well, then slowly pour on milk, stirring briskly all the time. Remove from heat, add egg yolks one at a time, beating well in between, then add courgettes/zucchini. Lastly add parsley, salt and pepper. Beat egg whites stiffly and fold into soufflé mixture. Pour into a well-buttered 2 pint (1.2 litre) soufflé dish and bake at 190 °C (375 °F/Gas 5) for 30 to 40 minutes, until well risen and a deep brown on top. Serve at once.

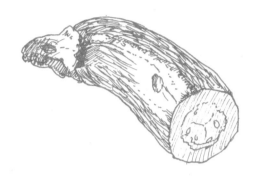

Speedy Cooked Courgettes/ Zucchini

These are simple to prepare and very good to eat. It is tempting to leave the courgettes/ zucchini in the juice to marinate for a short time while other parts of a meal are prepared, but don't. They really are best prepared at the last minute. For 2 people you will need 4–5 firm courgettes/zucchini, ½ teaspoon grated orange peel, 2 teaspoons – ½ oz (15g) approx. – butter, 2–3 tablespoons orange juice, salt and freshly ground black pepper, to taste and, if liked, 2 teaspoons of chopped fresh parsley or mint to finish. Heat a frying pan and add all the ingredients except the herbs. Stir-fry for 3 to 4 minutes, then sprinkle with herbs and serve at once – straight from the pan.

Courgette/Zucchini Quiche

This is one of the most delicate and delicious mixtures for a quiche.

Line a 9 in (22.5 cm) tart tin with short-crust pastry (see page 86). Bake blind at 190 °C (375 °F/Gas 5) until just beginning to colour, about 15 minutes, then remove from oven and leave to cool.

Serves 6

FILLING
6–8 medium courgettes/zucchini
1½ oz (45 g) butter
1 teaspoon chopped fresh thyme
1 tablespoon chopped spring onions
1 tablespoon currants, washed and dried
6 oz (185 g) curd cheese
4 egg yolks
6 fl oz (185 ml) single (light) cream
1 level teaspoon ground cinnamon
salt and pepper, to taste

Wipe courgettes/zucchini clean and slice thinly, preferably on a mandoline or in a food processor. Heat butter in a large frying pan over a low heat, add courgettes/zucchini and stir-fry for 1 to 2 minutes, then add herbs, spring onions and currants, mix gently, remove from heat and set aside.

Beat together curd cheese, egg yolks, and cream in a mixing bowl, add spice, salt and

pepper, then gently fold in the courgette/
zucchini mixture and pour all into the pastry
base. Bake at 180 °C (350 °F/Gas 4) for 30 to
40 minutes, until the centre of the quiche is
firm. Cover with a piece of greaseproof paper
if the top begins to brown before the quiche
is cooked. This quiche top should remain
pale in colour.

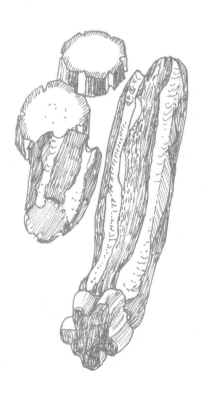

Courgettes/Zucchini with Rice

A complete meal. You will need only a crisp green salad to finish with. The combination of rice and just-crunchy courgettes/zucchini is wonderful. Do use a good olive oil and Italian risotto rice to get the best flavours and finish with this dish.

Serves 4

8 oz (250 g) Arborio or other suitable rice

5–6 fl oz (155–185 ml) olive oil

1 small onion, chopped

8 fl oz (250 ml) dry white wine

salt and freshly ground black pepper, to taste

20–30 fl oz (625–940 ml) hot vegetable or chicken stock

6–8 courgettes/zucchini, depending on size

1–2 cloves garlic, finely chopped

1–2 tablespoons roughly chopped fresh basil leaves (if possible)

Place rice in a fine sieve and wash well under the cold tap, the water should run clear when the rice is clean; shake well. Heat 3 fl oz (90 ml) of the oil in a heavy-bottomed saucepan with a tight-fitting lid, add onion and fry gently for 5 minutes; do not brown. Add rice and stir-fry for 2 to 3 minutes. Pour in the wine and add salt if stock is unsalted, then pour in 20 fl oz (625 ml) of the hot stock. Cover tightly, turn down heat to very, very low and leave the rice to cook undisturbed for 10 to 15 minutes, after which time lift the lid and add more hot stock if necessary. Cover and finish cooking; the grains of rice should be firm and separated.

While the rice is cooking prepare the courgettes/zucchini. Wipe clean and slice into ½ in (1 cm) rounds. Heat remaining oil in a frying pan, add garlic and courgettes/zucchini and stir-fry for 3 to 5 minutes, depending on size and age of courgettes/zucchini. Add salt and freshly ground black pepper. Now tip the whole lot into the rice, mix very gently together, cover and leave to stand off the heat for 1 to 2 minutes to allow flavours to blend, sprinkle with basil and serve at once.

Into mynde come to vs the goordis and the peponys, and the leeke, and the vniowns.
(1382, John Wyclif)

Courgettes/Zucchini with Cream & Ham

A quick, easy and very tasty dish. Try it for a summer lunch or light supper. All you need to accompany it is a dish of plain boiled or steamed new potatoes.

Serves 4–5
1½ lb (750 g) courgettes/zucchini
3 oz (90 g) butter
2 tablespoons chopped fresh parsley
1 tablespoon chopped chives
4 fl oz (125 ml) double (heavy) cream
8 oz (250 g) chopped cooked ham, or
collar, or gammon
salt and pepper, to taste

Wipe courgettes/zucchini clean and slice into diagonal slices, not too thick. Blanch in boiling water for 4 to 5 minutes – 3 minutes is

enough if very young and fresh. Drain and dry on absorbent kitchen paper. Melt the butter in a large frying pan, add courgettes/zucchini and stir-fry over a medium heat for 3 to 4 minutes. Add herbs, cream, ham, salt and pepper, increase heat and bring to the boil, stirring all the time. Boil for 1 minute, then serve straightaway. The courgettes/zucchini should still be crunchy and the herbs fresh tasting. You could part-cook this dish and finish it off at the last minute if you blanch in advance but it won't taste quite so fresh and good.

Stuffed Courgettes/Zucchini

Stuffed courgettes/zucchini are excellent and versatile: the same recipe often being equally suitable for serving hot as a main dish or cold as a starter or salad.

Serves 4–5
1–2 tablespoons cooking oil
1/2 small onion, chopped
6 oz (185 g) lean beef or pork, minced
1 tablespoon roughly chopped walnuts
1 tablespoon chopped fresh parsley
2 teaspoons chopped capers
salt and pepper, to taste
1–2 fl oz (30–60 ml) milk
2–2 1/2 courgettes/zucchini per person
6 fl oz (185 ml) water

SAUCE
10 fl oz (315 ml) thick (Greek-style) plain yogurt
10 fl oz (315 ml) single (light) cream
1 tablespoon finely chopped spring onions

To make the stuffing, heat oil in a frying pan, add onion and fry gently for 5 minutes, do not brown. Add minced meat and stir-fry for a further 5 minutes, then turn into a mixing bowl, add walnuts, parsley and capers and mix well. Season with salt and pepper, mix again, then add enough milk to make a firm stuffing. To stuff the courgettes/zucchini, cut courgettes/zucchini in half lengthwise and hollow out the seeds and some of the soft flesh. Fill hollows with stuffing mixture. Place on a baking dish, pour water round (not over), cover with foil and bake at 190 °C (375 °F/Gas 5) for 25 to 35 minutes, until the flesh is soft and the stuffing cooked. There should be almost no water left at the end of the cooking.

To make the sauce, heat together all the ingredients in a saucepan, do not boil. Pour round the courgettes/zucchini just before serving.

If you wish to serve these cold, do not heat the sauce but mix together and pour round the courgettes/zucchini while they are still warm, cool and serve. Hot new potatoes and a cucumber salad tossed in vinaigrette make good accompaniments.

Alternative Stuffings

Suggestions for alternative stuffings for courgettes/zucchini or small squashes or peeled and sliced vegetable marrow rings:

6–8 oz (185–250 g) cooked chicken
2 oz (60 g) cooked long-grain rice (1 oz (30 g) uncooked weight)
1 tablespoon chopped spring onions
1 tablespoon chopped walnuts
1 tablespoon chopped fresh parsley
salt and pepper, to taste

Mix all the ingredients together and proceed as above.

A Vegetarian Stuffing

8 oz (250 g) curd cheese
3 egg yolks
1 tablespoon chopped spring onions
1 tablespoon chopped fresh parsley
1 tablespoon chopped fresh mint
2 teaspoons chopped fresh thyme
salt and pepper, to taste

TOPPING

*2 tablespoons breadcrumbs mixed with 4
tablespoons finely grated cheese*

Mix all the stuffing ingredients well together,
stuff the courgettes/zucchini and proceed as
above. Ten minutes before end of cooking
time, sprinkle with the topping.

Lamb & Courgette/Zucchini Casserole

Serves 4

about 3 tablespoons olive oil
2 lb (1 kg) cubed lamb, preferably from leg
1 clove garlic, chopped
juice of 1 lemon and 1 orange
salt and pepper, to taste
4–6 courgettes/zucchini, depending on size
grated peel of 1 lemon
1 tablespoon chopped fresh parsley
2 tablespoons chopped fresh mint

Heat 2 tablespoons of the oil in a pan with a tight-fitting lid, add lamb and garlic and stir-fry for 10 minutes. Stir in lemon and orange juice, add salt and pepper, cover tightly and cook for 25 to 30 minutes, until lamb is tender but not overcooked.

While meat is cooking, slice courgettes/zucchini into rounds, ¼ in (0.5 cm) thick. In another pan heat about 2 teaspoons olive oil, add courgettes/zucchini and stir-fry for 5 to 10 minutes, until just cooked but still crisp. Sprinkle with lemon peel and chopped herbs and spoon over lamb. Serve at once.

Note: This dish can be reheated but the courgettes/zucchini will lose some of their crispness. If you want to make it in advance,

42

it is better just to cook the meat and leave the frying of the courgettes/zucchini until the last minute.

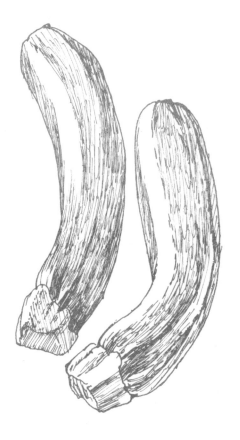

SUMMER SQUASHES

These vegetables are a joy to the eye: they grow in curious and beautiful shapes, from the slender and elegant, dark green courgette/zucchini to the beautiful, pale, scallop-shaped patty-pan squash, so pretty raw and so wonderfully exotic looking when served, yet simple to cook. These once un-usual vegetables have taken the place of the vegetable marrow on our tables and indeed are as easy to find as that poor, benighted vegetable. But don't despise the marrow:

picked young and carefully cooked, it can be as good as any of our other, now more popular, summer squashes.

The most prolific of these latter is the hybrid crookneck, which is bulbous at the blossom end and grows to about 8 in (20 cm) in length. Other summer squashes are mostly round, oval or onion-shaped and are eaten small – about tennis ball size.

Crookneck

Askutasquash, their Vine aples, which the English from them call Squashes, about the big-nesse of Apples, of severall colours, sweet, light, wholesome, refreshing.

(1643, Roger Williams 'A Key into the Language of America')

Butternut Squash with Basil Starter

Best made a day ahead, if possible. For a starter use one medium-sized squash per person.

Cut squashes in half, remove seeds and brush with olive oil. Place in a baking dish, cover with foil and cook in a moderately hot oven, 190 °C (375 °F/Gas 5) for 25 to 35 minutes, until cooked but very firm to touch. Uncover and set aside.

For 4 squashes make up the following dressing:

6 fl oz (185 ml) white wine
4 tablespoons best olive oil
1 tablespoon white wine vinegar
1 clove garlic, crushed
3 tablespoons basil leaves, torn up by hand
salt and pepper, to taste

Mix all the dressing ingredients well together. Cut squash halves in four while still warm, pour over dressing and leave to marinate. Serve cold.

A dearth caused them to fall upon their pompions, squoshes etc, before they were ripe.
    (1764, Thomas E Hutchinson 'The History of the Province of Massachussetts Bay')

Butternut

Patty-Pan

These are the prettiest of vegetables to serve; you will need one per person. They can be boiled or baked whole, the tops removed, the seeds scooped out and the hollow filled with a nut of butter, or a butter sauce, or a mixture of rock salt, pepper and a teaspoon of chopped fresh herbs.

To bake whole, wrap in foil and bake at 190 °C (375 °F/Gas 5) for ¾ to 1 hour.

To boil, trim stalk, cover with boiling water, add salt and cook gently for ¾ to 1 hour, test with a skewer.

They can also be stuffed and baked. To do this, cut off the tops, remove seeds and fill the hollows with a favourite stuffing. The curd cheese recipe for stuffed courgettes/zucchini (page 41) is particularly good. Bake as above.

Baked Squash & Onions
Good with fried bacon and sausages.

Serves 4–5
2 crookneck squashes
2 onions
2 apples
2 oz (60 g) butter, melted
salt and pepper, to taste
*6 fl oz (185 ml) single (light) cream, to
finish*

Remove skin from squashes if at all tough,
then slice into ¼ in (0.5 cm) rounds. Slice
onions and apples and layer with squashes in
an ovenproof dish. Pour over melted butter,
sprinkle with salt and pepper, cover with foil
and bake at 190 °C (375 °F/Gas 5) for 30 to
40 minutes. Remove foil, pour over cream
and bake uncovered for a further 10 to 15
minutes.

Great Pumkin, its fruit striated, round, but somewhat flattish, mixt with white and red, but within yellow.

(1729, William Dampier 'A New Voyage Round the World')

Custard Marrows/Squashes

These respond to simple cooking. Peel, cut off the top and remove the seeds. Add a nut or two of butter, season with salt and pepper, wrap in foil and bake at 190 °C (375 °F/Gas 5) for 1 to 1¼ hours.

They ain't got two ideas to bless themselves with, the stupid, punkin-headed, consaited blockheads!
(1835, Thomas C Haliburton 'The clockmaker, or the sayings and doings of Samuel Slick of Slicksville')

Marrow & Ginger Soup

Serves 4–6

2 oz (60 g) butter

1 onion, chopped

4 lb (2 kg) marrow, peeled, seeded and chopped

1 in (2.5 cm) piece of fresh ginger root, peeled and grated

20 fl oz (625 ml) white stock

10 fl oz (315 ml) milk

10 fl oz (315 ml) cream

salt and pepper, to taste

a dusting of ground ginger or cinnamon, to serve

Heat butter in a large pan, add onion and fry gently for 5 minutes, do not brown. Add marrow and ginger and stir-fry for 5 minutes, then pour on stock, cover and cook for 20 minutes. Purée in a blender or food processor, return to pan, stir in milk, cream, salt and pepper, reheat and serve with a dusting of ginger or cinnamon.

Vegetable Marrow with Egg

Like courgettes/zucchini, the younger the marrow, the better the flavour. This recipe is suitable for a marrow 8 to 10 in (20 to 25 cm) long. When as young as this, the vegetable should not need to be peeled.

Serves 4–5

2–3 oz (60–90 g) butter, plus extra for greasing

1 marrow, sliced in ¼ in (0.5 cm) rounds, seeds removed

2 tablespoons chopped chives

2 tablespoons chopped fresh mint

4 eggs

6 fl oz (185 ml) single (light) cream

salt and pepper, to taste

Heat butter in a large frying pan and gently fry marrow rings for 2 to 3 minutes on each side. Butter a 2½ pint (1.5 litre) baking dish, lay marrow rings in it and sprinkle with herbs. Lightly mix together eggs and cream in a bowl, add salt and pepper and pour over the marrow. Bake at 180 °C (350 °F/Gas 4) for 30 to 40 minutes or until egg mixture is set.

Two dishes peculiar to New England, toast dipped in cream and pumpkin pie.

(1818, J Palmer 'Journal of Travels in US')

Baked Vegetable Marrow

It is essential to use young marrows of 8 to 10 in (20 to 25 cm). This is not a stuffed marrow, the breadcrumbs and herbs simply give flavour to this unusual dish.

1 marrow

2–3 oz (60–90 g) butter, plus extra for greasing

2 oz (60 g) breadcrumbs

2 teaspoons chopped fresh thyme

1 tablespoon chopped spring onions, white part only

salt and pepper, to taste

Wipe marrow, trim ends and cut in half lengthwise. Remove seeds and any soft spongy flesh, then cut marrow pieces in half crosswise. Melt 2 oz (60 g) of the butter in a small saucepan and use to brush marrow pieces liberally. Grease an ovenproof baking dish

with butter and lay the pieces of marrow in it, skin side down. Place, uncovered, in the oven and bake at 190 °C (375 °F/Gas 5) for 15 minutes.

While marrow is cooking, put breadcrumbs in a small mixing bowl, add the last 1 oz (30 g) of the butter to any remaining in the saucepan, melt and pour onto the breadcrumbs. Add herbs, spring onions, salt and pepper and mix lightly together keeping the mixture crumbly – this is not a stuffing. Remove the marrow from the oven and sprinkle liberally with the breadcrumb mixture, then return to the oven and bake for a further 15 to 20 minutes. Eat straight from the shells with a spoon as you would eat an avocado.

This is also very good without the breadcrumbs: dust with salt and freshly ground black pepper after the first 15 minutes of cooking and paint with more butter.

Patty-Pan

Pompion or Pumpkin, a sort of Fruit of the nature of melons.

(1706, Edward Phillips 'The New World of English Words, or, A General Dictionary')

Deep Fried Marrow Rings

Young vegetable marrow is delicious deep fried – slice the marrow into rounds, remove the seeds, dip in melted butter and deep fry until puffed up and golden. Alternatively, dip in seasoned flour, beaten egg, then breadcrumbs and fry in a mixture of butter and cooking oil, 5 minutes each side. These marrow rings are delicious served with a homemade tomato sauce, such as the ones on pages 85 and 86, or topped with grated cheese and browned under the grill.

Marrow & Apple Chutney

This recipe could use older marrows – some of the giants from the gardening show would do very well for this delicious chutney.

2 lb (1 kg) marrow, peeled and seeded

2 lb (1 kg) cooking apples, peeled and cored

8 oz (250 g) onions

2 oz (60 g) crystallized ginger

12 oz (375 g) brown sugar

15 fl oz (470 ml) white wine vinegar

dried root ginger, about $^{3}/_{4}$–1 in (2–2.5 cm) long

$^{1}/_{2}$ oz (15 g) whole cloves

3 blades mace

1 dried chilli pepper

Chop marrow and apples in cubes about 1 in (2.5 cm) in size, they need not be equal. Finely chop onion and crystallized ginger

Vegetable Marrow

and place in a large pan with marrow and apple, then add sugar and vinegar. Tie root ginger, cloves, mace and chilli in a muslin bag and add to the pan, place over a gentle heat and bring to the boil, stirring all the time, then reduce heat and simmer for 1½ to 2 hours, or until the chutney is thick. Remove the muslin bag of spices, cool slightly and pot in clean, dry jars (see page 87), cover and store on a cool dry shelf. This chutney, like most chutneys, is best kept for 3 months, more if you can, before eating.

WINTER SQUASHES

These tough-skinned vegetables store well and are an excellent addition to our winter diet. Like summer squashes, they come in beautiful shapes and colours: the lovely, brilliant green and yellow Turk's Turban is a good example. As many of these squashes can be boiled or roasted whole, they not only make a pleasant change from the more usual winter vegetables but also are an exciting new visual experience on the table. In general they are best cooked simply and served with melted butter or a light sauce. Small varieties make delightful and unusual starters and give the cook very little work. They are also excellent as light lunch or supper dishes.

Apart from those for the giant pumpkin, the recipes are generally interchangeable – begin by experimenting with a small baked squash.

Pumpkin

Baked Acorn Squash

One squash will serve 2 to 3 people. Simply wipe clean, cut in half lengthwise – do not remove the seeds. Place in a baking dish and bake at 190 °C (375 °F/Gas 5) for 45 minutes to 1 hour. Now remove the seeds, dust with salt, add a good grinding of black pepper, fill the centres with a nut of butter and serve at once. You could make a beurre blanc sauce instead, for a treat, see page 80.

Baked Winter Squash

Most winter squashes bake well, either whole, wrapped in foil, or in halves as in the above recipe, the drier squashes are best wrapped in foil before baking.

Boiled Winter Squash

Wipe or wash the squash, cut in half, then into slices and peel the slices: 2 lb (1 kg) prepared weight will serve 4 people. Remove the seeds and stringy pieces, place in a bowl in a steamer, pour on one cup of water and add 1 oz (30 g) butter and salt to taste. Cover tightly, steam for 10 to 15 minutes, until just tender. If you are not using a steamer but a saucepan, you may need to add a little more water during the cooking but squash is best cooked in as little water as possible. Drain well, add another 1 oz (30 g) butter and some freshly ground black pepper and serve at once.

If you like, you can mash the squash together with a little cream and a pinch of ground mace, ginger or cinnamon.

Squashes are a small sort of Pumpkin, lately brought into request.

(1707, John Mortimer 'The Whole Art of Husbandry')

Winter Squash Purée

This is very good. Use one of the medium-sized squashes, such as Golden Delicious or Queensland Blue. Wipe clean, wrap tightly in foil and bake at 190 °C (375 °F/Gas 5) for 1½ to 2 hours, until tender. Remove the foil, cut off the top of the squash and scoop out the fibrous centre and seeds, then purée the flesh in a blender or food processor. Transfer to a saucepan, add 2 oz (60 g) butter with salt and pepper to taste and reheat gently.

Serve with grilled bacon in a casserole, or on its own, sprinkled with grated cheese and accompanied by a salad.

It is exceedingly curious to behold the Wild Squash climbing over the lofty limbs of the trees.

(1791, William Bartram 'Travels through North and South Carolina')

Pumpkin

Pumpkins

These vegetables with their wide range of sizes have many more uses for our winter table than merely that of a humble pie filling. Although still not as popular as the squash, the pumpkin is re-emerging as an important ingredient in our winter range of vegetables. A 5–6 lb (2.5–3 kg) pumpkin, which serves 4 people comfortably and is generally known as a pie pumpkin, is good baked or boiled. Larger varieties slice and fry or steam and make good soups and purées.

Spiced Pumpkin Soup

This soup is best made with all milk. The apple lightens the taste and texture.

Serves 6
2¹/₂ oz (75 g) butter
2 lb (1 kg) prepared pumpkin, cubed
1 onion, chopped
¹/₄ teaspoon curry paste or powder, or to taste
20–30 fl oz (625–940 ml) creamy milk
1 large cooking or tart apple, peeled and chopped
salt and pepper, to taste

Melt 2 oz (60 g) of the butter in a large saucepan over a gentle heat, add pumpkin and onion and stir-fry over a low heat for 5 to 8 minutes, do not brown. Add curry paste or powder, pour on milk and simmer very gently for 30 to 45 minutes, until vegetables are tender. Melt remaining butter in a small pan and gently fry apple until tender. Strain pumpkin and onion, reserving liquor and place fruit and vegetables in a blender or food processor. Process to a fine purée, then return to the pan and reheat with the cooking liquor and season with salt and pepper.

A single pumpkin could furnish a fortnight's pottage.
(1833, Leitch Ritchie 'Wanderings by the Loire')

Gold Nugget Fries

These squashes are at their best when about 5 in (12.5 cm) in diameter. Try them fried. For 4 people you will need 2–3 squashes.

2–3 squashes
flour, for coating
salt and pepper, to taste
pinch of ground nutmeg
1 egg, beaten
2 oz (60 g) butter

TO SERVE
plain yogurt or sour cream
chopped spring onions
chopped fresh herbs

Peel squashes, remove seeds and slice lengthwise. Mix together flour, salt, pepper and nutmeg on a plate or shallow dish. Dip squash slices first in flour, then in beaten egg, then again in flour. Melt butter in a large frying pan, add squash and fry until brown on both sides, 3 to 4 minutes per side. Serve with a bowl of yogurt or sour cream to which you have added some chopped spring onions and fresh herbs.

An empty gourd in which the shrivelled beans of
the world's spent pleasures were shaken.
(1873, Pascerèl 'Ouida (Mlle L de La Ramée);
only a story')

Sliced Baked Squash I

There are many variations of this dish; this is
the simplest: 1½ lb (750 g) squash will serve
4 as a vegetable accompaniment.

Wipe, peel and slice the squash into
serving-sized pieces. Butter a shallow baking
dish, arrange the slices in it and pour over
2–3 oz (60–90 g) of melted butter to which
you have added salt and pepper to taste.
Cover the dish with foil and bake at 190 °C
(375 °F/Gas 5) for 1 hour, or until tender.

Sliced Baked Squash II

Proceed as above but pour over 4 fl oz
(125 ml) double (heavy) cream before baking. You can flavour the cream with chopped
chives, spring onion, parsley, tarragon or
fresh marjoram, alternatively, add a tablespoon of chopped, cooked ham or bacon,
fried and crumbled.

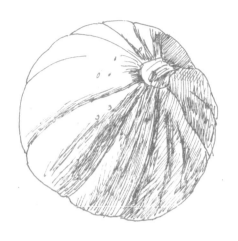

Small Winter Squash, Baked

These bake well whole, you don't need to wrap them with foil but bake as for jacket potatoes. Some of these small squashes have a delicious nutty flavour.

Baked Stuffed Squash

The very pretty squash, Turk's Turban, so aptly named, has a good flavour for baking plain and whole or stuffed. Try any of the courgette/zucchini stuffings given on pages 38 to 41 and serve with a bowl of thick plain yogurt, to which you have added a little milk or cream. The average squash of about 6 lb (3 kg) will serve 6 people and take 1½ to 2 hours to bake at 190 °C (375 °F/Gas 5).

Main Course Baked Squash

Serves 4–5

2 lb (1 kg) squash, peeled, seeded and sliced thinly

4 spring onions, chopped

4 rashers best bacon or gammon, not too thin

1 lb (500 g) tomatoes, skinned and sieved to a purée

2 egg yolks, beaten

3 fl oz (90 ml) double (heavy) cream

salt and pepper, to taste

2 tablespoons breadcrumbs

2 tablespoons chopped fresh parsley

Butter a 3½ pint (2.25 litre) shallow baking dish liberally. Arrange sliced squash inside, sprinkle on spring onions and lay bacon on top. Mix tomato purée with egg yolks and cream in a bowl, add salt and pepper and pour over bacon and squash mixture. Mix together breadcrumbs and parsley and sprinkle over the dish. Bake at 190 °C (375 °F/Gas 5) for ¾ to 1 hour, until squash is tender and top brown. If top gets too brown, cover with greaseproof paper or foil.

Goordes rawe be vnpleasant in eatinge.
(1533, Sir Thomas Elyot)

SWEET SQUASH RECIPES

This section is not concerned with a particular variety of squash; it is simply a short selection of recipes for creams, puddings and a marrow jam.

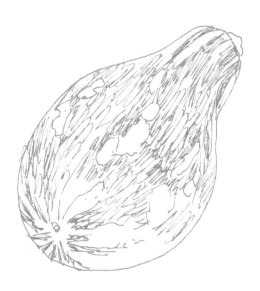

The prickly and green-coated gourd,
So grateful to the palate.
(1784, William Cowper 'The Task')

Marrow Cream

Good on toast or as a cake filling. If you make lots, turn some into a delicious pudding with fresh orange slices.

2 lb (1 kg) marrow, peeled and seeds removed

juice of 2 oranges

4 oz (125 g) butter

2 lb (1 kg) sugar

2 teaspoons grated orange peel

2 tablespoons chopped preserved ginger

Chop marrow into 1½ in (4 cm) cubes. Place in a heavy-bottomed saucepan with orange juice, cover tightly and cook gently for 8 to 10 minutes until tender, shaking pan occasionally to prevent sticking. Add butter, sugar, orange peel and ginger and cook very slowly over a low heat for 30 to 40 minutes. Beat well. Pour into sterilized jars, cover and seal, see page 87. Use as for lemon curd. It is best stored in the fridge, where it will keep for 2 to 3 months.

Baked Sweet Squash

Try this with some of the nutty-flavoured small squashes or stuff one of the larger squashes and bake whole. If baking little squashes whole, cut off the tops after cooking, remove seeds and fill with a mixture of sugar, cinnamon, butter and/or cream. Alternatively, scoop out the hot sweet pulp and eat with ice cream.

To Stuff a Squash with Sweet Stuffing

Choose a nicely shaped squash, not too large, and fill it with the following stuffing. The dried fruit should be soaked overnight.

Serves 6–8
1 medium squash
4 oz (125 g) dried prunes, stoned
4 oz (125 g) dried apricots
4 oz (125 g) dried figs
1 oz (30 g) candied mixed peel
1 teaspoon grated lemon peel
1 teaspoon grated orange peel
1 oz (30 g) butter, cut into pieces
1 oz (30 g) brown sugar

Cut the top off the squash and remove seeds and stringy pulp. Chop dried fruit roughly, mix with grated peels, butter and sugar and use to fill the squash. Replace the 'lid', wrap in foil and bake at 190 °C (375 °F/Gas 5) for 1 to 1½ hours.

To serve, remove foil and lid, place in a serving dish, cut into wedges and serve with a spoonful of the stuffing. Spice biscuits and thin cream are a good accompaniment.

Pumpkin Pudding

Pumpkin pie is a combination of textures which I don't care for, but the filling makes a good dish on its own without the pastry. Try serving it with a well-flavoured apple purée or, better still, with a fresh orange fruit salad.

Serves 4

1 lb (500 g) pumpkin, weighed after slicing, peeling, removing seeds and chopping roughly

10 fl oz (315 ml) cream

3 eggs

4 oz (125 g) sugar

2 teaspoons orange peel

1 teaspoon ground ginger

1 teaspoon ground cinnamon

1/4 teaspoon ground cloves

To prepare the pumpkin purée, cook in 1/2 cup water until just tender. Drain well, then purée in a blender or food processor without adding any of the remaining cooking liquor. Beat together cream, eggs and sugar in a mixing bowl, add orange peel and spices and beat in the purée. Pour into a 1 1/2 pint (1 litre) greased baking dish and bake at 180 °C (350 °F/Gas 4) for 30 to 40 minutes, or until the pudding has set. Serve warm or cold with stewed fruit or a fresh fruit salad.

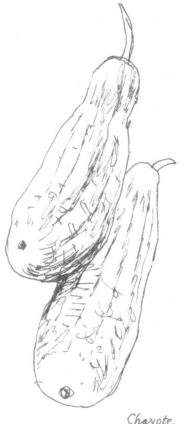

Chayote

Pumpkin Soufflé

A hot spiced pudding enriched with candied peel and nuts.

Serves 5–6
2 oz (60 g) butter
2 oz (60 g) plain flour
2 teaspoons mixed spice
grated peel of 1 lemon
2 fl oz (60 ml) medium sherry
2 fl oz (60 ml) milk
1 lb (500 g) pumpkin, puréed (see above)
4 eggs, separated
4 oz (125 g) sugar
2 oz (60 g) candied mixed peel
2 oz (60 g) chopped raisins
2 oz (60 g) chopped toasted hazelnuts, see page 88

Melt butter in a saucepan, remove from the heat, add flour and mix together to make a roux. Stir in spice and lemon peel, then blend in sherry, milk and purée, beating well to break down any lumps. Return the pan to the heat and cook, stirring continuously, until the mixture thickens. Remove from the heat, beat in egg yolks, one by one, then stir in sugar, candied peel, raisins and hazelnuts. Beat egg whites stiffly, then fold into pumpkin mixture and pour into a well-buttered 3 pint (1.75 litre) soufflé dish. Bake in a hot oven 190–200 °C (375–400 °F/Gas 5–6) for 30 to 45 minutes, until well risen and mixture has set. Eat at once.

Butternut

The Seed Note

And don't forget the pumpkin seeds: these can be washed, dried and salted. Dry them by gently frying, then sprinkle with salt. Though small, the seed is also worth shelling, for it's very tasty. Children will eat them straight from the fresh vegetables.

Marrow Jam

Don't be tempted to use old, large marrows for this once very popular country preserve. If the vegetables are old and dry, the jam will not set. The jam is no longer much made, which is a pity, for it is mild and mellow and makes a pleasant alternative to marmalade for breakfast.

3 lb (1.5 kg) marrow, weighed after peeling and seeding
½–¾ teaspoon salt
3 lb (1.5 kg) sugar
juice of 2 lemons
6 oz (185 g) crystallized ginger, finely chopped

Cut marrows roughly into 1–1½ in (2.5–4 cm) cubes, place in a bowl, sprinkle with salt, toss well and cover with a clean cloth. Leave for 12 hours or overnight. Next day, strain off the salty water, sprinkle sugar over marrow and leave for another 12 hours or overnight. Next day, turn into a preserving pan and stir in lemon juice and ginger. Bring slowly to the boil and boil until the marrow is quite translucent and the juice reaches a light set, see page 87. Marrow jam is slow to reach a set, the cooking time varies from 30 to 45 minutes, and it doesn't 'jell' hard. Pot in clean, dry jars, see page 87, cover and store on a dry shelf.

SAUCES &
ACCOMPANIMENTS

Many recipes for squashes, marrows, pumpkins and courgettes/zucchini are simple.
When, for example, they are baked whole in
their skin and a sauce or dressing is all that is
required to enhance their flavour. Some
squashes can be dry and stodgy and are
therefore best served with a dressing or
sauce which is not flour-based. Yogurt,
cream and mayonnaise-based sauces are all
good with hot or cold vegetables of the
cucurbitaceae family. The recipes given here
are suitable for 4 people.

Classic Beurre Blanc

This French sauce usually served with fish is not difficult to make and is excellent served with any of these hot cooked vegetables. The sauce is traditionally made using shallots but you can use a small sweet onion instead or, for a very delicate sauce, you can omit the onion altogether. Work with cold butter. I have deliberately left out the tablespoon of thick cream most recipes use, as the sauce works perfectly well without it.

10 oz (315 g) butter, preferably unsalted:
if using salted do not add salt
6 fl oz (185 ml) dry white wine
1 tablespoon white wine vinegar
2 shallots or 1 small onion, finely chopped
salt and pepper, to taste

Chop butter into 1 in (2.5 cm) cubes and keep cool until you are ready to use it. Place

wine, vinegar and shallots in a 1½ pint (1 litre) saucepan, bring to the boil and boil rapidly until only 1 tablespoon of the liquor remains. Remove from the heat and begin to beat in the butter, a piece at a time, using a balloon whisk or an electric beater, until it is thoroughly incorporated into the wine mixture. This is rather like making a mayonnaise, so watch carefully for oiliness and curdling. Keep the pan near a low heat as you add the butter. When all the butter is added, season with salt, if using, and pepper. Serve as soon after finishing as possible – it should be warm only – and do not reheat.

This sauce can be flavoured with herbs if you like – try adding 2 tablespoons of chopped fresh parsley, chives or tarragon at the end.

Classic Greek Lemon Sauce

Very good with all bland vegetables.

3 egg yolks
juice of 1–2 lemons
10 fl oz (315 ml) white stock
salt and freshly ground black pepper, to taste

Beat together egg yolks and juice of 1 lemon in a large mixing bowl. Bring stock to the boil and pour onto the egg and lemon mixture, whisking all the time. Return the mixture to the pan and very gently reheat, taking care not to boil and stirring continuously with a wooden spoon. Taste for lemon seasoning and add more juice if liked, then season with salt and pepper. This sauce should be warm rather than hot.

Orange & Lemon Sauce

This sauce is no classic and has no pretensions to anything other than being quick to prepare.

2 oz (60 g) butter
juice of 1 orange
juice of 1 lemon
1 teaspoon grated orange peel
1 teaspoon grated lemon peel
1 tablespoon chopped chives
1 tablespoon chopped fresh parsley
salt and pepper, to taste
1–2 teaspoons wine vinegar, if desired
1–2 teaspoons brown sugar, if desired

Melt butter in a saucepan and when it begins to bubble, add orange and lemon juice. Return to the heat and boil for ½ to 1 minute, then add grated peels, herbs, salt and pepper. Vinegar can be added at this stage if a very tart sauce is required and sugar too, if liked.

*A selected seed of Squash, which is an Indian
kind of Pompion, that Growes a pace.
   (1661, Robert Boyle 'The Sceptical Chymist')*

Fresh Tomato Sauce

This can be used hot or cold. If using hot,
gently heat and serve at once: do not allow to
boil as the lovely fresh taste is lost with too
much cooking.

*1 lb (500 g) ripe tomatoes, roughly
chopped*

2 tablespoons dry or medium sherry

*1 teaspoon onion juice (made by squeezing
a piece of onion in a garlic press)*

salt and pepper, to taste

pinch sugar, or to taste

Place all ingredients in a blender or food
processor and process until smooth, then
press through a sieve to remove pips and
skins.

*Candied apple, quince, and plum, and gourd.
   (1820, John Keats 'The Eve of St Agnes')*

Cooked Tomato Sauce

For use when a hot, well-flavoured sauce is required.

2 fl oz (60 ml) olive oil
2 onions, roughly chopped
2 cloves garlic, chopped
2 lb (1 kg) tomatoes, skinned
2–4 tablespoons tomato purée or paste
salt and freshly ground black pepper, to taste

Heat oil in a large saucepan, add onions and garlic and stir-fry for 5 minutes, do not brown. Add tomatoes, cover and simmer for 30 to 40 minutes, then add tomato purée or paste, salt and pepper. If a really thick sauce is wanted, uncover 15 to 20 minutes before end of cooking time.

BASICS

Plain Shortcrust Pastry
Suitable for savoury and sweet tarts.

8 oz (250 g) flour
1/2 teaspoon salt
4 oz (125 g) butter or margarine, hard and cold
3–4 tablespoons ice-cold water

Sift flour and salt into a mixing bowl. Cut fat into flour using two knives or a pastry cutter and mix briefly in a food processor or rub in with fingertips. When mixture looks like breadcrumbs, add water and draw together; the mixture should be very stiff. Knead together against the sides of the bowl, then wrap in plastic wrap and leave in a cool place or the bottom of the fridge for 30 minutes or until you wish to use it. If left for several hours or overnight, the pastry should be brought to room temperature for 2 to 3 hours before use.

To Test Jam for Set

Remove saucepan or preserving pan from heat and put a little jam or jelly onto a cold plate. Leave to cool, then tilt the plate slightly. The jam is setting if it begins to wrinkle at this point.

If using a sugar thermometer, 'set' is reached at 110 °C/220 °F.

To Pot Jam, Curd or Preserves

Potting must be done correctly to keep food from developing bacteria.

Make sure that the jars are completely sterile, warm and dry. Remove any foam that may have formed on the surface of the liquid and pot carefully and quickly. Fill jars to the brim, cover with wax circles, then seal with self-sealing lids. Label and store in a cool, dark place or the fridge, as directed.

To Toast Hazelnuts Easily

Heat a dry, clean frying pan, pour in the nuts and 'toast' dry over the heat. When the nuts are dark brown all over, tip into a sieve and rub off the skins. Do not chop until cold. You can prepare more of these than you require as they will keep for 4 to 6 weeks if stored in a screw-topped jar in a dry place.

Storing & Freezing

Winter squashes and some pumpkins store very well indeed. Lay out on clean newspapers, straw or in baskets in a cool, dry, airy place, taking care they do not touch each other. Check occasionally for mould or shrivelling. Use as you would the fresh-picked fruit.

Marrows, squashes, pumpkins and gourds are not really suitable for freezing fresh. They can be frozen in purée form but the flavour is lost after only a very short time.

INDEX

90

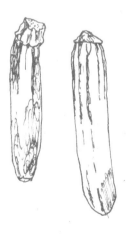